Food For

~~Lazy~~ Busy People

Simone Bocedi & Claudio Santori

You Can Make It
Helsinki, Miami

Published by: You Can Make It
www.youcanmake.it

Instagram: @foodforbusypeople

To Rosanna and Loretta, our mothers,
infinite sources of love and good cooking.

Content:

Introduction

Our philosophy applied to cooking

Too many people believe that cooking tasty food is far more complicated than it is. Cooking delicious recipes is surprisingly easy, affordable, and fast if you only commit to putting in the discipline of trying, experimenting, and trying again.

No matter if you're an expert chef or have never set foot in the kitchen before, this book will give you incredibly tasty and healthy recipes you can easily prepare. Most of them take less than 25 minutes. We will also share how to wash the dishes in no time, as it only takes a couple of minutes if you do it right.

Hi! We are Simone and Claudio. Since the day we randomly met in Helsinki, Finland, more than 15 years ago, there hasn't been a week we haven't talked about food, sharing recipes, videos, tricks, and tips. Both born and raised in Italy, we love eating healthy food without compromising on taste.

We are busy with our jobs, families, children, and projects, and knowing how to cook a few quick, tasty dishes has been incredibly valuable. It has helped us stay on track with our health and fitness goals and enjoy the added benefits of developing a fantastic skill: cooking and feeding the people around us with great food.

We see cooking at home as an essential part of our lives. This is why we gathered a few of the recipes we love most –those which have helped us lose weight, stay fit throughout the years and made our families happy.

Overall, we'd like you to *try and fail a lot*. It's the only way to learn how to cook. If you miss an ingredient, it's going to be ok, and the dish will still taste good, just exchange it for another ingredient or simply cook without it. It's a learning process. This is also the reason why *we did not put any measures*. 100 grams of chicken? 250 grams? It doesn't matter. Three tomatoes? Four? Who cares! Try and see! It's called "Food for ~~Lazy~~ Busy People", not "Gourmet Michelin Chef Recipe Book".

Play along, and you'll be making tasty recipes starting today.

What's different about Food for ~~Lazy~~ Busy People?

We bought more than 100 recipe books in our lifetime, and many are great and at the same time not so great. Exotic ingredients, complex procedures, and so many tools! You would have to clean your kitchen for a week. In this book, the recipes are so easy that you can't mess them up.

We believe in creativity and adaptability. You can personalize most of the recipes however you prefer when you don't have one of the ingredients. You can even leave the food cooking while you're on the phone with a friend for a few extra minutes. It will still taste amazing.

For starters, this book has **flexible and changeable ingredients.** We have read many books and blogs, tried hundreds of recipes from apps, Reddit and YouTube, and the most annoying parts were usually two: very strict measurements and rare (which often meant expensive) ingredients. The recipes you'll find in this book have flexible components. Some people prefer saltier dishes, others can't stand salt but love spices. Some like broccoli, others are spinach friends.

What if we told you that it doesn't really matter how much or which ingredients you put as long as you follow the main instructions? That if you put 2 instead of 3 potatoes, it's still going to taste pretty much the same?

Also, we chose easy and common ingredients, which you will most likely find in the nearest corner store. You won't ever find any rare ingredients here, no algae nor duck liver, like in some fancy recipe books. And this is most certainly NOT a fancy recipe book: it has the words ~~LAZY~~ BUSY PEOPLE in the title!

On top of the simplicity, this is a collection of recipes **you can't screw up,** not even if you tried. You can exchange a few ingredients here and there, and even overcook or undercook a meal by a 20% margin, and they're still going to taste fantastic –just different.

We want to make it as easy as possible for you to choose one recipe, cook it, enjoy it, and go on with your day without having to waste a whole afternoon in the kitchen or at the food store looking for a specific ingredient you'll only need once. Our ingredients reappear in many recipes on purpose.

Can I really prepare these recipes, cook and wash the dishes in less than 25 minutes?

These are really fast recipes to prepare, and most of them can be prepared and cooked in less than 25 minutes, including cleaning the kitchen. However, some of them will need to sit in the oven for a while, but the preparation is still so easy you'll wonder: "How is it even possible?"

Others might take a few more minutes to prepare and cook, but none of them require you to stay an hour in the kitchen other than because you really want to.

A recipe book with no pictures?

We don't want to use professional pictures of the recipes. We both work in marketing and trust us: many of the professional food pictures you see online are fake. We've helped chefs and private companies have their dishes photographed. We hired food stylists (yep, that's a job), who use a lot of chemicals and different sprays to make the dishes look shiny, perfect… and quite unreal.

We even starred in commercials for TV, and every time we had to pretend to eat the meals in front of us: the actual food was too poisonous to touch after they made it look pretty for the camera.

Life isn't perfect, and food images shouldn't be either. Instead of doing photoshoots and using photoshop to give you an impossible ideal to meet, we wanted to do it as real as possible. What it means is that we want to use *real images from real people who have cooked these recipes*. For that, we will use Instagram @foodforbusypeople. If you take the time to prepare one of our recipes, **tag us on Instagram @foodforbusypeople,** and we might repost you with full credits to your @username. Together, we can create a feed with real images from real people.

What is *Healthy?*

Almost every cookbook claims to be full of healthy recipes. We want to make an agreement and tell you upfront what we mean by "healthy":
- Lots of vegetables in every meal
- High-quality fat
- Highly nutritional food (not just empty calories)
- A moderate amount of carbohydrate (easy to personalize based on your diet)
- Medium to high amounts of proteins
- No processed food (or as little processed food as possible)
- No added sugar
- No refined grains, for the most part, or easy to substitute
- Little to no cheese, or easy to substitute
- Easy to digest by most people

As we already mentioned, we prefer recipes with only a few natural ingredients you can find in your local grocery store. We tried to avoid recipes that have a variety of too many ingredients we don't know their source.

Most importantly, the recipes in this book are great for a long-term strategy to get (or keep) a lean body. They will also help you keep your energy levels high at all times, from the moment you wake up until you go to sleep.

With the freedom of flexible ingredients, this is a Paleo / Vegan / Pegan / Ketogenic / Vegetarian / Low-Carb recipe book.

We all agree sugar is bad, processed food is terrible, and we should eat a lot of vegetables. So, at the end of the day, we're arguing about beef vs tofu, pork vs soy, chicken vs legumes. **Feel free to choose your proteins**, whatever you believe is healthier for you or the environment.

We won't lie to you: we would probably eat pizza and pasta every other day. It would make our Italian mothers happier. But the energy in our bodies depends on what we eat every day.

There's no way around it: if you don't eat well, you will end up overweight, feeling bloated, and with low energy, making it difficult to have the necessary vitality to accomplish everything you want from life.

Also, eating at restaurants or take-aways are great and easy, and we do it sometimes, too.

The problem with food you don't prepare yourself is that you really don't know what ingredients they're using, how much oil, sugar or flour they're using, and you're often paying not only with your money but also with your energy.

Our goal for this book is to limit processed food and cook a healthy meal at home in the least amount of time, without sacrificing nutritional value and flavor.

PART I — HOW TO

Cooking is fun when you know how to do it. The next few pages are full of tips to make cooking fun. Forget about all the stress and the negative emotions you might have related to preparing meals, cooking them, or cleaning after.

Embrace this culinary journey with a smile on your face, follow these tips, and you'll be an expert in no time.

Preparing — the art of starting right

Start every dish by putting **everything you'll need on the counter.** It will make your life much easier. This includes tools, ingredients, the recipe you want to cook, and a timer. It also makes for a great starting picture on the Instagram Story of your dish.

Wash the fruit and vegetables under cold water.

Slice, peel, and cut all the ingredients before you start. It may add a couple of minutes to the recipe preparation, but it'll save you some stress while preparing the recipe, especially in the beginning. Later on, you will learn how to multitask between cutting and cooking.

Keep the **trashcan nearby** so you don't have to move around and keep opening and closing the lid. Alternately, we set a small bowl on the counter to quickly dispose of everything before the final journey to the trash bin.

Cooking – where the magic happens

Set timers so you won't forget something's cooking (or not cooking). Use your phone, Siri, Google Assistant, or even Alexa, to set a timer without using your hands.

Heat the skillet before putting oil in it. You'd know it's the right temperature when you place a drop of water in it, and it'll move around sizzling a bit before evaporating. Wait until the oil is hot before adding any ingredient or food. This is useful for many reasons, the most important one is it will help the food not stick to the pan.

In the beginning, **taste your food a lot**. It's the only way you'd get better at cooking: understanding what is needed to get to the flavors you like.

Preheat the oven when requested, and remember to turn it off once you're done cooking.

Use accessories to hold hot skillets and plates, or to take things in and out of the oven. Cooking scars are great stories to tell, but we hope you'd have better stories while keeping your skin safe. Whatever you use, make sure it's not wet. A wet towel will get hot instantly and potentially burn you.

Take pics and share them with your friends. If you put them on Instagram, remember to **tag us: @foodforbusypeople.**

Cleaning – as if nothing ever happened

Always rinse dishes and tools as soon as you're done using them. If you rinse them immediately, it'll only take a few seconds to clean them, and you won't end up scrubbing cookware and utensils with hardened stains or for an hour.

Consider using a **brush** instead of a sponge. It's convenient since you can use hot water and avoid using gloves. If you have a **dishwasher**, use it. It's that simple. Rinse everything before putting the utensils into the dishwasher. You should also wash the dish brush in the dishwasher once a week, placing the brush (bristle-end up) in the cutlery holder. Oh, and buy **environmentally friendly soap**, please, thank you.

If you have a small kitchen, consider buying an extra bucket to rinse and wash the dishes. You can find online some handy **collapsible wash basin (google it)**. Fill the foldable bucket with warm water and soap before you begin cooking, then throw everything in. When you're ready to wash, all you have to do is a simple brushing and rinsing of the cookware and utensils under hot water. Clean dishes in no time!

Ingredients — matching your diet

Here's a list of ingredients we frequently use when we cook, and a few ways to replace them. Prefer unprocessed whole foods. If your ingredients come inside a box or a can, get accustomed to reading their nutritional values and you'll soon find out which macros fit your diet and lifestyle better.

Oil

In the recipes, we often refer to it as just "Oil". Pick the one you want and like the most, based also on your beliefs and diet. Some recipes might taste slightly different when using a different kind of oil, but as we said already, it's your job to try, experiment, and find the right combinations you enjoy.

Extra Virgin Olive Oil: Great when cold and to garnish food with, but not so good for cooking, especially at high temperatures.

Olive Oil: Perfect for cooking. It can be used cold, too.

Coconut Oil: Great for cooking at high temperatures. For some people, it leaves an aftertaste they're not used to.

Avocado Oil: Same as coconut oil, but it doesn't leave a strong aftertaste.

Proteins

Meat & Fish: the best proteins you can find, unless you are a vegetarian/vegan. They're also a great source of fat and they don't contain too many carbohydrates (which turn to sugar!). Try to buy grass-fed meat and wild fish. Your body and the environment will thank you.

Soy & soy-derived products: You can modify almost all recipes, including meat or fish, with soy-derived products. Use your favorite vegetarian/vegan proteins, and you're all set.

Beans & Cheese are also rich in proteins. Be careful with their carbohydrate & fat values.

Vegetables

Vegetables are often interchangeable and it's ok to experiment, mix and match different ones. Be creative. If you bought aubergines instead of zucchini, it's okay. If you start a recipe and you only have a carrot when the recipe calls for bell peppers, try it out!

Clearly, if you are making a Spinach Risotto and you don't have spinach, you will end up making something else, but you never know, it might even be better than the original recipe! **Experiment!**

When cooking vegetables, you have to remember that different vegetables cook at different times. How to solve this problem? Add the vegetables at different times, in the right sequence. Chop them bigger or smaller depending on whether they take a shorter or longer time to cook when putting all together at the same time.

Try things out, taste, experiment. Try again.

Tools — the essential gear

Fewer tools = lesser complex process & fewer things to clean at the end.

We try to minimize the number of tools needed when cooking.

The ones listed below are all the general tools you need and will find inside this book, except for occasional exceptions.

A Sharp Knife

It might sound counterintuitive, but the sharper your knife is, the less likely it is to cut yourself. Most of the accidents in the kitchen happen when using a non-sharpened knife: the knife slips when applying unnecessary pressure and ends up in places it shouldn't, like your fingers. We don't want that, so we always buy the best knives we can afford.

Suggested: A vegetable peeler is also the easiest, safest way to peel the skin off of vegetables.

Cutting Board

This makes it much easier to cut the ingredients without ruining your kitchen counter and tables. Cutting boards also make it easier to clean up after you're done preparing. Silicon or plastic ones are not only reusable but washable in the dishwasher. Highly recommended.

Use a plate as an alternative, if needed.

Frying Pan

Or skillet. It's very convenient to stir-fry vegetables and proteins (meat, soy, beans...you name it).

Fry: raw food is immersed in oil and cooked for a long time. Frying is not so good for your health.

Stir-Fry: you add a thin layer of oil and cook proteins and vegetables for a shorter time while stirring.

Buy a **non-stick** pan or a ceramic one. Go for the highest quality you can afford. They're not that expensive, are easy to clean, and not harmful to health. If you use a low-quality one, you'll spend a lot more time cleaning up after or be at a higher risk of eating some toxic chemicals from the pan. A good skillet can last you up to 10+ years!

Note: Never use a steel/metallic tool with a non-stick pan! Use wood, silicon, or plastic only. If you scratch the pan, you should replace it. If you don't have a pan, use a pot or a saucepan.

Oven

An oven makes it easy to cook food while you do something else.

Preheat the oven, as it takes a few minutes to reach the right cooking temperature. Place the food inside only when the oven is at the correct temperature (there's usually a light indicator).

Set a timer when you have food sitting in the oven as it's too easy to forget it. **"Hey Google, Set a timer for 25 minutes!"**. Your phone, Siri, Alexa, and Google Assistant are very helpful in this.

Remember to use protection for your hands when removing objects from the oven, they are HOT! And switch off the oven when you're done cooking.

Extra tools for the oven:

- Cooking is easier with greaseproof paper. It's cheap, and it will save you time cleaning after you're done cooking.
- Use pot holders to not burn your hands.
- Use tongs to hold/turn the food in the oven.

Pot with a lid

A big pot means we can prepare soup to last for an entire week in just one sitting.

Suggested: Use a saucepan or frying pan with a lid as a replacement.

Bowls

We use bowls for salads, whisking eggs, and mixing ingredients.

Suggested: Use pots and plates as replacements.

Utensils: spoon, spatula and tongs

These three are the most essential kitchen tools to mix, stir, grab, and turn your ingredients. Metal utensils scratch frying pans, so we'd avoid them. Whether wood, silicon or plastic, buy the best quality you can afford.

Blender

A blender is incredible, as you can chop vegetables, prepare sauces, and prepare soups. Blenders are easy to clean and extremely safe to use.

Suggested: As a replacement, use a knife or boil vegetables and mash them with a fork.

PART II – The Recipes

You finally made it to the juiciest part of the book. What you'll find next are the most incredible recipes of your life. They're incredible for so many reasons. First of all, they're **quick to prepare**. Second, they're really **easy**. Third, they ARE **delicious**. Fourth, most of them can be easily modified to become **vegetarian, vegan, paleo, low carb, keto**, while keeping the heart and soul of the original recipe. You don't have to follow any particular order, and even though some recipes are easier than others, you can pick a random recipe, and you won't fail. Simply cook what inspires you most.

The book starts with the **Magical Side Dishes**, which are quick meals to impress anybody, perfect as appetizers or side dishes. **Crack 'em!** is all about eggs. **Enjoy the Snack** will become your go-to food while watching movies or the easy snack you pack for a picnic or road trip. They're great for quick meals! The same goes for **Smoother Than a Smoothie**, where we reveal our all-time favorite smoothie recipes.

One Meal, One Love are quick to prepare, will feed an entire family, and you won't need to cook anything else for that day. **Prepare In a Minute, Check Back Later** are technically not done within 25 minutes, but in reality, they are super quick to prepare and you can just leave them cooking in the pot or in the oven while you enjoy life.

We wanted to give you extra variety, so here comes **Mamma Mia, Che Pasta!** Yes, you guessed it. These are the best pasta sauces our mothers cooked for us. If you're not into carbs, or gluten, you can always find great alternatives for pasta like zucchini-noodle, rice noodle, or gluten-free pasta.

We conclude the book with a collection of the best risottos we've ever cooked: **Masterclass: Risotto.** Rice is not low-carb, but if you're ok with it, these are delicious and perfect for your cheat-meal. Risottos are also a little bit more advanced than the other recipes, but the effort pays off in taste.

If you take the time to prepare one of our recipes, we would love it if you could show us the result (or the preparation!). Just **tag us on Instagram @foodforbusypeople.**

Buon appetito!

Magical Side Dishes

In this section, you'll find a collection of side dishes. While they won't fill you if you're really hungry, these dishes are easy to prepare, will help stave off the hunger, and will greatly complement your main courses.

True to its name, these side dishes will tease your taste buds —a thrilling intermission for the highlight of the meal.

Soutéed Vegetables

Time: 5' prep + 12 cook + 3' clean

This is the side dish we enjoy together with many of our warm meals. It's as easy as a salad, just... warm. Our favorite combination for this recipe is bell peppers, zucchini and rosemary, which are the ones stated here below. However, we suggest you go to your local supermarket and experiment with different substitutes. The combinations to bring this dish to life are numerous and the joy of cooking will come with trying different options. Soon enough you'll find out which one is your favorite.

INGREDIENTS:

- Zucchini (or any veggie substitute)
- Bell peppers
- Onion or garlic
- Rosemary (or any preferred herb)
- Salt & Pepper
- Oil

DIRECTIONS:

1. Finely chop the onion or the clove of garlic and set aside.
2. Finely chop the vegetables, add them to a bowl with a dab of oil, salt & pepper, and mix.
3. Heat a drizzle of oil in a frying pan and add the onion or the garlic.
4. When the onion or garlic are golden (and not burnt), add the vegetables to the pan, and stir.
5. The vegetables' liquids should be enough to cook them in, but you can always add a little bit of water to add steam and avoid burnt food.
6. While the vegetables cook, clean the bowl you used before. This is also a good time to set the table.
7. After 12-15 minutes, the vegetables will be "the right kind of soft". The only way to find out your "soft" level is to taste them, experiment and learn! Serve warm.

Make it extra: You can add parmesan cheese when serving to make it even richer in taste.

Holy Guacamole

Time: 8' prep + 0' cook + 2' clean

Every time we serve guacamole, we think "we should do this more often". It's rich in taste and a perfect companion for both meat and fish. Our take on it is the spicy version, but just remove the peppers for a version that's palatable to all. As with the rest of our recipes here, you're encouraged to use measurements that are more suited to you as preferences in taste vary for us all. Experiment and you'll find the right amounts for you in no time.

INGREDIENTS:

- Avocados
- Small red onion
- Fresh cilantro
- Lime juice
- Salt & pepper
- Chili peppers, seeded

DIRECTIONS:

1. Cut the avocados in half, discard the pits.
2. With a fork, mash the avocados in a bowl.
3. Finely chop the onion and cilantro, add into the bowl.
4. Do the same with the peppers. Be careful! You can use disposable gloves to cut the peppers to avoid nasty surprises later when touching your eyes or mouth with peppered fingers.
5. Add the lime juice, salt & pepper, and with a fork mash until it has a consistency that you like.

Make it extra: Try adding small pieces of tomatoes at the end for an alternative, chunkier version.

Simple Tzatziki

Time: 5' prep + 0' cook + 2' clean

We learned this super easy, keto-friendly version of Tzatziki in Crete, Greece. Whenever we cook lamb, this is a sauce we love to prepare as a simple side dish, sauce to the salad, or to pour directly over the meat. It's sweet and fresh because of the yogurt.

INGREDIENTS:

- Greek yogurt (substitute with almond or coconut yogurt for a vegan version)
- Garlic
- Salt & Pepper
- Cucumber
- Oil
- Lemon juice (if you have it)

DIRECTIONS:

1. If you have time, you could strain the yogurt with a coffee filter for an hour or so, to remove any excess liquid. When we're in a hurry we skip this step and the result is equally delicious.
2. Scoop the seeds out of the cucumber, then grate it with a cheese grater and place inside a metal strainer.
3. Sprinkle with salt and push it down with a spoon to remove any excess liquids.
4. Crush the garlic and combine it with all the ingredients in a bowl and mix.
5. Garnish it with black pepper and oil.
6. If you have time, place it in a fridge for an hour before serving, but again, the result is very good even when you serve it immediately.

Make it extra: Do you love spicy? You could add fresh and finely cut chili peppers to it!

Roasted Brussels Sprouts

Time: 8' prep + 20' cook (unattended) + 3' clean

The concentration of vitamins in a cup of Brussel sprouts should make you want to eat these vegetables multiple times a month. You'll get half the recommended amount of Vitamin C, plus great amounts of Vitamin A, K and potassium. Did we convince you yet?

INGREDIENTS:

- Brussel sprouts
- Salt & Pepper
- Oil

DIRECTIONS:

1. With a small knife, take the tip off the stem, and the first layer of outer leaves.
2. Depending on the size of the Brussel sprouts, cut them in half or into ¾ parts. Not too small though, or they will burn easily when roasting.
3. Place them on parchment paper on the oven pan and drizzle with oil.
4. Season with salt & pepper and mix a bit.
5. Cook at 375°F / 180°C for 20 minutes.

Make it extra: You can add garlic and parmesan cheese and any herbs you like before roasting to make it even richer in taste.

34

Fresh Tomato Fennel Salad

Time: 8' prep - 0' cooking - 2' clean

This two-ingredient salad is a hit every time we serve it. It's fresh, summery, delicious, crunchy and soft all at the same time. The combination of tomatoes and fennel is something you really want to try. Oh, and did we say it's super easy to prepare?

INGREDIENTS:

- Tomatoes
- Fennel
- Salad dressing (Salt, Pepper, Oil, whatever you wish!)

DIRECTIONS:

1. Wash both vegetables under cold water.
2. Open the fennel leaves with your hands and then cut into small cubes, and add to a bowl.
3. Cut the tomatoes as well into small cubes, and add to the bowl.
4. Season with salt & pepper and any oil you like.
5. Serve cold.

Make it extra: Garnish it with herbs such as parsley or spring onion. It'll add great flavor and color. With the white of the fennel, the red of the tomato, and the green of the onion spring you have now created the Italian flag! Congratulations!

Bell Peppers Souté with Balsamico

Time: 5' prep + 3' cook (active)
+ 15' cook (unattended) + 3' clean

Here's another side dish that's easy to make and yet tastes like a fancy restaurant.

INGREDIENTS:

- Bell peppers: red, orange, yellow, green ...the more colors, the better looking the dish will be.
- Onion
- Salt & Pepper
- Oil

DIRECTIONS:

1. Cut the bell peppers into thin strips or squares, and set aside.
2. Heat a drizzle of oil in a skillet and add the finely chopped onion to it.
3. When the onion is golden, add the bell peppers to the pan, and stir.
4. Now add a little bit of water to increase the steam and avoid burnt peppers. Cover with a lid.
5. After 12-15 minutes, the peppers will be "the right kind of soft".
6. Add a swirl of balsamic vinegar and stir for half a minute on high heat.
7. Season with salt & pepper and serve warm.

Make it extra: Garnish with any herbs you like. Try rosemary, parsley, thyme or any other to your liking. We also like to add fresh arugula to mix the tastes and create a completely new side dish from the same starting point.

Mystical Dates

Time: 10' prep + 5' cook + 3' clean

We stumbled into this recipe and from then on we can't live without it. It's our go-to when we have guests coming as it's fast to prepare and very quick to cook. Great for when you want to serve something before the main dish is ready.

INGREDIENTS:

- Dates
- Parma ham
- Basil
- Walnuts
- A soft cheese, if you like

DIRECTIONS:

1. If you're planning to cook them right away, turn on the oven at 375°F / 180°C.
2. With a knife, start with a small cut on the dates just enough to remove the pits.
3. Stuff the dates with walnuts and a bit of soft cheese – if you like.
4. Gently close up the dates and wrap them with basil and ham.
5. Arrange them on a baking sheet, ready to cook.
6. Put the tray into the oven and keep it there for 5 to 10 minutes.
7. Enjoy how delicious this is. Sweet and salty blending together!

Make it fun: Ask your guests what they think the ingredients are and they'd never guess it!

Stuffed Mushrooms

Time: 3' prep + 15' cook + 2' clean

Stuffed mushrooms are like little presents for anyone eating with you. They'll open these and not quite know what to expect. Surprise them! Make them differently from one another, also to see and learn which ones you like the most.

INGREDIENTS:

- Large mushrooms
- Any filling (e.g. bell pepper, ham, egg, grated zucchini)
- Not an ingredient, but you'll need aluminum foil or baking paper to bake them in

DIRECTIONS:

1. Turn on the oven and set to 350°F / 180°C.
2. Wash the mushrooms then rip off their stems.
3. Holding the mushroom upside down, you can now fill it up with anything you like.
4. Cover the mushroom in foil, making sure no liquid comes out.
5. Bake for about 10-15 minutes.
6. Serve immediately.

Make it extra: Try adding gorgonzola to the filling. Not so healthy, but so yummy!

Easy Vegan Cauli-rice or Couscous

Time: 5' prep + 0' to 3' cook + 3' clean

If someone were to tell our 15-year-old selves that we will enjoy eating so much cauliflower, I would have thought them crazy. And yet here we are, enjoying cauli-rice every week. Cauli-rice is light, fluffy, tasty, takes only 5 minutes to make (cold version) or 10 minutes (warm). It can replace rice or couscous as a side dish –and it turns out that kids like it, too!

INGREDIENTS:

* Cauliflower
* Salt & Pepper
* Oil

DIRECTIONS FOR COUSCOUS COLD & WARM:

1. Coarsely chop the cauliflower and put it in the blender.
2. Blend and it's ready to serve, raw and crunchy, seasoned with any added herbs and salt & pepper.
3. If you prefer it warm and softer, heat a drizzle of oil in a frying pan, add the blended cauliflower and cook for a couple of minutes.

DIRECTIONS FOR RICE:

1. Break the cauliflower with your hands or with a grater. You can cut the core with a knife.
2. Heat a drizzle of oil in a skillet.
3. Add the cauliflower, cover with a lid, and cook for 3 minutes.
4. Season with any herb, salt & pepper, and serve.

Make it extra: Add any cheese on top of the warm version.

Shishito Peppers

Time: 2' prep + 20' cook (not active) + 2' clean

A delicious side dish requiring close to no preparation. While some shishito peppers can be spicy, they are the perfect side for a lot of dishes.

INGREDIENTS:

- Shishito Peppers
- Salt
- Olive Oil

DIRECTIONS:

1. Preheat the oven at 380°F / 190°C.
2. Wash the shishito peppers and place them on a tray.
3. Sprinkle with salt and olive oil and mix with your hands.
4. When the oven is ready, put them in.
5. Keep in the oven for 20 minutes.

Make it fun: One shishito pepper will be super, super, super spicy. Whoever gets it wins!

Paleo Bacon-Wrapped Asparagus

Time: 8' prepare + 15' cooking (unattended) + 2' clean

We like to have this paleo appetizer alone or together with a fresh salad.

INGREDIENTS:

- Asparagus
- Bacon
- Pepper

DIRECTIONS:

1. Preheat the oven at 400°F / 200°C.
2. Cut off the woody end of the asparagus. Keep the rest and wash under cold water.
3. Cut the bacon in thin strips.
4. Wrap the bacon strips around each single asparagus, making sure they don't overlap too much.
5. Place the asparagus on a baking sheet over a wire rack (better for airflow) or a baking pan and bake for 15 minutes or until the bacon is crisp.
6. Upon serving, season with black pepper. While the asparagus bake, this is a good time to either clean the cutting board and knife you used or carry on with the rest of the meal.

Make it extra: More like, "extra step". If you want, you could flip the bacon-wrapped asparagus mid-way the baking, so they cook evenly on both sides.

Crack 'em!

Eggs, eggs, more eggs, and then some more. If you like eggs, then you'll be mesmerized by these tasty recipes.

As most of the recipes in this book, pretty soon you'd only use them as templates to start experimenting with your favorite ingredients; and fried eggs will never be the same again.

Who knew that an ingredient as ordinary and as common as eggs can add rich flavor and flair to your meals! Let's dive in.

Ultimate Keto Scrambled Eggs

Time: 2' prep + 10' cook (active) + 3' clean

Once you try these incredibly soft eggs, you'd never want them scrambled any other way. The secret to success here is to keep an active eye on the eggs and stir repeatedly. You'll serve real chef-level eggs in less than 15 minutes –including cleaning.

INGREDIENTS:

- About 2 eggs per person (or freely decide your preferred quantity per person)
- Butter
- Fresh cheese or mayonnaise
- Salt & Pepper

DIRECTIONS:

1. Set the pot on the stove (don't turn on the fire yet).
2. Put some butter and crack the eggs on top.
3. Turn on the stove.
4. When the eggs start turning white lift the pan, mix the ingredients, and put it back on the stove.
5. Repeat lifting, mixing, re-setting for a few minutes. The whole point is to not let them cook too much.
6. While it's still cooking, add salt & pepper and a bit of fresh cheese (or mayonnaise) and mix. This will help the eggs remain soft.
7. Once you see that it's getting less soft, turn off the stove and serve.

Make it extra: It adds a lot to the styling (and will impress your partner) if you chop chives and sprinkle it on top before serving. But, as said, it's just an option for a touch of cuteness. And, who keeps chives in their kitchen anyway? We usually buy it once in a while, cut it into small pieces, and freeze them. They're ready to use whenever.

Egg Muffins

Time: 5' prep + 15' bake + 10 clean

Warm or cold and whether for busy mornings or a quick bite on your way to a meeting, these salty egg muffins are customizable with whatever flavor you like –and are great for any occasion. You can prep them in no time. Low carb and keto-friendly, the only challenge you have is getting a muffin pan or silicon liners to bake them in. We've tried paper liners and they get stuck. If you can't get silicon liners, grease the muffin pan to avoid sticky annoyances.

INGREDIENTS:

- 10 eggs (12 muffins)
- Salt & Pepper
- Any filling you like

DIRECTIONS:

1. In a large bowl, break the eggs, add salt & pepper to taste, and whisk everything.
2. Grease the muffin pan and pour the mixture into the muffin molds. Do not overfill! Fill each tin only about 2/3 full.
3. Add whichever filling you like.
4. Bake at 400°F / 200°C for about 10-15 minutes.
5. Once golden, remove from the oven and set aside to cool.
6. You can store them in plastic bags or reusable containers in the fridge. Stick them in the microwave for 30 seconds to reheat and enjoy!

Make it extra: Top them with your favorite spices and herbs (chili peppers, thyme, basil ...be creative!)

Just Eggs Omelette

Time: 1' prep + 8' cook + 3' clean

Using eggs in so many ways can sometimes feel almost overwhelming. But, omelette is one of those simple, yet savory, dishes you can cook in many different ways. Here's the basic recipe: just with eggs.

INGREDIENTS:

- Oil / Butter
- Eggs (about 2 per person or freely decide your preferred quantity per person)
- Salt & Pepper

DIRECTIONS:

1. In a pan, heat a drizzle of oil or a knob of butter.
2. Break and whisk the eggs in a bowl and when the pan is hot, add the eggs in the pan.
3. From one side, gently push the outer cooked parts of the eggs towards the center and the uncooked parts will now flow into the empty side of the pan.
4. When the omelette is half-way cooked (and pay attention, it's fast!), with the spatula, place one half over the other half. Now, the omelette should cover only half of your pan.
5. Cook for a minute more, then serve.

Make it extra: Garnish it with a few herbs if you can. We find chives to be the best one, but you can be creative.

Any Kind Omelette

Time: 2' prep + 8' cook (active) + 3' clean

One of those customizable recipes, omelette is a versatile dish that's generous enough to allow you limitless creativity. What can you put inside an omelette? Pretty much anything! From bacon to mushrooms, feta to cheese, ham to cheddar cheese (or, why not both?). That's right. It's highly customizable you can come up with any omelette creation you want! The only caveat? Fillings should be ready to eat. If they're not (like bacon), you have to cook them separately before you start.

INGREDIENTS:

- Oil / Butter
- Eggs (about 2 per person or freely decide your preferred quantity per person)
- Salt & Pepper
- Filling ingredients (if you want)

DIRECTIONS:

1. In a pan, heat a drizzle of oil or a knob of butter.
2. Break and whisk the eggs in a bowl and when the pan is hot, put the mixture in the pan.
3. From one side, gently push the outer cooked parts of the eggs towards the center and the uncooked parts will now flow into the empty side of the pan.
4. When the omelette is half-way cooked (and pay attention, it's fast!), cover half of the omelette with any filling you like.
5. Here's where you'll feel like a chef. With the spatula, fold the half with no filling over the half that's covered by ingredients. Now the omelette should cover only half of your pan.
6. Cook for a minute more, then serve.

Make it friendly: If you have many people to serve, make several omelettes (it only takes 5 minutes) – rather than make one big one. With several omelettes, you can customize each one and they'll be fluffier and simply better because they're way easier to handle. Also, each person will feel extra special since you took care of them individually.

Spinach Frittata

Time: 2' prep + 10' cook + 5' clean

Frittata is a variation of omelette. What's the difference then? Whereas with omelette you add egg first, here you cook it all together for a little bit longer. Oh, and it can be served cold, too. We've also been having frittata as a snack during the day.

INGREDIENTS:

- Olive Oil / Butter
- Onion
- Spinach (or grated zucchini)
- Salt & Pepper
- Eggs (about 2 per person or freely decide your preferred quantity per person)
- Grated cheese (if you have it)

DIRECTIONS:

1. Heat the oil or a knob of butter.
2. Cut the onion into small pieces and add them to the pan.
3. When the onion is golden, add spinach.
4. Add a bit of water to the mix so the vegetables won't burn.
5. While the spinach cooks, whisk the eggs with salt & pepper and grated cheese.
6. When the spinach is cooked, add them to the same bowl with the eggs and mix vigorously.
7. Pour the mix back in the pan, and cover with a lid.
8. When you see that the sides are almost cooked, you can either turn the frittata upside-down with a plate, or cut the frittata in four, then turn every single piece with your spatula.
9. Serve when the crust is the right shade of brown you like.

Tip: You can exchange the veggies and even add meat to it. The combinations are numerous! You can also use more egg whites than whole eggs to make it richer in proteins, while dodging the fat and carbs.

Avocado Toast with Fried Egg

Time: 5' Prep + 3' cook + 2' clean

On the hunt for Instagram-worthy breakfasts? This is high on the list. It also helps that it's healthy and tasty.

INGREDIENTS:

- Avocado
- Oil / Butter
- Lime/lemon juice (if you have it)
- Eggs
- Salt & Pepper
- Chives / Dried chili peppers to garnish (if you have them)
- Whole-grain Toast

DIRECTIONS:

1. Cut the avocados in half and discard the pits. With a fork, mash the avocados in a bowl.
2. Add a little bit of lime or lemon juice and salt & pepper to the bowl.
3. Place a pan on the stove at medium heat. Add very little oil or a knob of butter to it.
4. In the meantime, toast the whole-grain bread and distribute the mashed avocado on it.
5. Crack the egg in the pan and let it cook for a minute. While you wait for the egg to cook, you can already clean the bowl.
6. When the egg starts to whiten below, turn it upside down with a spatula. Add salt & pepper to taste.
7. Fry until brown, then place on the avocado.
8. Garnish the toast with chives or dried chili peppers. Add extra black pepper on top if you like, serve warm.

Make it extra: You can add a layer of fresh cheese under the avocado. No more dairy-free but still incredible –and even more instagrammable.

One Meal, One Love

There's this tale in Helsinki about two Italians. Legend has it that those two, while out with friends on a Saturday night, would look at each other and silently agree on the next move. *"An after-party?"* *"No! Let's go home, make some lemon rice, and watch a great movie."*

There were numerous nights we spent making meals and watching episodes of *Lost* or *How I Met Your Mother* or just talking about life. Those are some of our most treasured memories together! It was, in a way, our expression of love for each other and our delight for life.

The message is potent and clear with every spoon of these One Meal, One Love dishes. These delicious entrées express nothing less than affection –whether for your partner, children, or friends. There's plenty of love to go around for as many people as you want.

These recipes are quick, easy, and sufficient for an entire meal –without needing a side dish or second dish. You can even increase the number of ingredients so that you can save a pot or two for other meals. These recipes give you plenty of food for one day or more!

Vegetable Cake

Time: 15' prep + 15' cook (supervised)
+ 30' bake (unattended) + 5' clean

This is by far one of our favorite vegetable dishes –which can easily be turned into a side dish. It's one of those "let's see what I got in the fridge and cook 'em" recipes. The standard version has only 4 ingredients, but you can mix and match and try out different versions with other vegetables, such as sweet potatoes, carrots, aubergines, and broccoli.

INGREDIENTS:

- Onion
- Zucchini
- Potatoes
- Carrots
- Oil
- Parmesan cheese (if you have it)
- Salt & Pepper
- Herbs, such as parsley or rosemary

DIRECTIONS:

1. Cut the onion, potatoes and zucchini in similar small cubes. Clean and slice the carrots in rounds.
2. Heat a drizzle of oil in a skillet and toss the onion in.
3. When the onion is golden, add the vegetables and stir. Add a little bit of water to increase the steam and cover with a lid.
4. While the vegetables sear, preheat the oven at 375°F / 180°C.
5. After about 15 minutes, when the potatoes start getting soft, you can move everything in a baking pan. Stir and season with salt & pepper and any herbs you'd like to add or try.
6. If you have some, you can also sprinkle parmesan all over it.
7. Bake for 25-30 minutes at 375°F / 180°C.
8. Let it cool for a few minutes and serve.

Make it extra: Make your version by substituting vegetables! Sweet potatoes, broccoli, Brussel sprouts, asparagus, different herbs... follow the steps but try your version of it.

Chicken & Broccoli Stir-fry

Time: 5' prep + 15' cook + 5' clean

Personal trainers all around the world suggest this meal as the ultimate 'healthiest full meal' any sporty person should eat. With over 40 proteins per serving, you can enjoy this lean meal multiple times a week.

INGREDIENTS:

- Boneless, skinless chicken
- Broccoli
- Onion
- Pepper
- Soy sauce
- Oil

DIRECTIONS:

1. Cut the chicken into thin strips, set aside.
2. Chop the onion and set aside.
3. Heat oil in a frying pan and add the onion.
4. Wait until the onion is golden, then add broccoli and a little bit of water to prevent the broccoli from burning. Cover with a lid.
5. Add the chicken and stir-fry until brown.
6. Pour soy sauce and pepper and stir-fry until the sauce is thick and the chicken well-cooked.

Make it extra: You can add other vegetables as well, like bell peppers.

Turkish Kisir

Time: 20' prep + wait until cold

One of our good friends from Turkey made this for a birthday party and, since then, it has turned into one of our all-time favorites when we have big gatherings with friends. Prepare beforehand and store in the fridge as it should be enjoyed cold.

INGREDIENTS:

- Bulgur
- Bell peppers (red, green, orange ...your choice!)
- Tomatoes
- Red onion
- Garlic
- Parsley
- Lemon
- Feta (if you have it)
- Olive oil
- Salt & Pepper

DIRECTIONS:

1. Put the bulgur in a pan and pour in water, about 2 fingers higher than the bulgur. Cook to boil.
2. While the bulgur cooks, chop all the ingredients into small pieces and put them in a large bowl (set the lemon aside).
3. Mix the bulgur with all the ingredients and add A LOT of olive oil, lemon extract, and some salt & pepper. Serve cold.
4.

Make it extra: If you add red paprika chili pepper paste, it turns into a completely new meal that's best for adults. And, why not some beef on the side?

Beef Stew

Time: 5' prep + 20' cook + 3' clean

A riot of flavors and another one of those recipes you can customize almost completely. The dish is great with white rice as a side dish.

INGREDIENTS:

- Ground beef
- Onion
- Bell Pepper
- Beans
- Tomato sauce (or fresh tomatoes)
- Salt & Pepper

DIRECTIONS:

1. Cut the onion and red peppers into very small pieces.
2. In a pot, add water measuring a couple of centimeters / one inch (about 1-3 glasses, depending on the pot and the glasses!)
3. Add the onion and peppers.
4. Turn on the heat and let it run for 5 minutes.
5. Add the ground beef and let it cook for 2 more minutes, stirring here and there.
6. Add beans and tomato sauce, stir, close the lid and let it cook for another 10 minutes.
7. Add salt & pepper to taste, and serve.

Make it vegan: substitute beef for soy meat.

Lemon Rice

Time: 5' prep + 10' cook (active) + 2' clean

This is a quick, tasty rice dish. You are going to prepare the lemon sauce while the rice is cooking. Perfect for winter and summer.

INGREDIENTS:

- White rice
- Lemon zest
- Egg
- Salt & Pepper

DIRECTIONS:

1. Boil the rice. Proportion: two cups of water for every cup of rice.
2. While the rice is cooking, put the egg into a bowl (one per person!).
3. Take one lemon and add the zest on top of the egg. You can add the peel, just try to cut it in very small pieces.
4. Add salt & pepper and mix it to make it look consistent.
5. Once the rice is cooked, remove the water and add it to the bowl. Mix the rice and the lemon sauce. Enjoy!

Make it extra: Add mozzarella and parmesan into the bowl if you prefer. And keep a bit of the hot water from the cooked rice, in case you need it to dilute the mixture.

Paleo Crispy Bacon with Veggies

Time: 5' prep + 15' cook + 2' clean

A lot of people make too many mistakes when cooking bacon. First, you don't need any extra oil as the bacon fat will do the work. Second, the secret to getting bacon perfectly crispy, but not too dry, is to add a half glass of water when the bacon is almost ready. And you can have it as a main dish for breakfast just by adding delicious veggies fried in bacon grease.

INGREDIENTS:

- Bacon
- Mixed vegetables (sauerkrauts, broccoli, spinach or whatever you want really)
- Pepper

DIRECTIONS:

1. Chop the vegetables you want to add before you start cooking so that they're ready when the time comes.
2. Put the skillet on the stove and when it's hot enough, add the bacon. You don't need extra grease. The bacon has all the grease you need to cook it.
3. When you hear them sizzle after a few minutes, turn the slices over to make them crispy on both sides.
4. When it's already turning brown and almost done, that's when you add the half glass of water.
5. When most of the water evaporates, place the slices of bacon on a plate covered with kitchen paper to absorb some of the grease.
6. Now the skillet is filled with bacon grease which we will use to cook some vegetables with. Remember that the bigger the pieces the longer it takes to cook, but it shouldn't take longer than 10 minutes.
7. When they're the right kind of soft, add pepper to the vegetable (the salt comes from the grease). Serve on a plate, placing the now crunchy bacon on top.

Make it extra: Fresh tomatoes and whole-grain rice make for great side dishes.

The Fridge Cleaner

Time: 5' prep + 10' cook (active) + 5' clean

This recipe is so easy and practical: we cook it every time we need to "clean" the fridge. This is a template we'll be using for a few more of our favorite variations of the protein-plus-vegetables theme.

INGREDIENTS:

- Any protein
- Random vegetables (carrots, zucchini, broccoli, sweet potatoes)
- Salt & Pepper
- Oil

DIRECTIONS:

1. Turn the fire on, and add some oil on the pan.
2. Stir fry the meat lightly until it turns brown (4-5 mins).
3. Stir frequently so it doesn't stick or burn.
4. While meat is cooking, chop the vegetables. The smaller the pieces, the lesser time it'll take to cook.
5. Add the vegetables. Remember that the bigger the pieces, the longer it takes to cook.
6. Add salt.
7. Cook until all the veggies are soft (they should easily cut in half when sliced with a spoon).
8. When serving, add olive oil and salt & pepper –as desired. Experiment with different veggies and vary the order of cooking them.

Make it extra: It's a fridge cleaner! Place other items that are running out, like fresh herbs or fresh vegetables for an even fuller taste.

Mamma Mia, Che Pasta!

Oh, wait a second, but the title said "healthy"! Is pasta even healthy? Well, we don't want all of our ancestors to come back from the dead and kill us for publishing a cookbook without pasta recipes! Nowadays, you can find gluten-free pasta made of lentils, chickpeas, or even broccoli. We even like to cut zucchini lengthwise or spiralize them to create what is called *zoodles*, a.k.a. zucchini-noodles.

Whatever your pasta or pasta substitute is, these sauces are great and we've been cooking them since we helped our mothers in the kitchen as kids.

So yeah, this part is for you, Mums!

Grandma Bolognese Sauce

Time: 3' prep + 15' cook (active)
+ 3 hours cook (unattended) + 5' clean

The reason Bolognese sauce has been so famous for so long is that it's incredibly simple to prepare and yet tastes so magnificently. When the sauce is simmering, the house is filled with smells and flavors that will transport you back to an old, forgotten Italy –just like what happened to the food critic in the film Ratatouille. Bolognese sauce is a perfect cook-and-store-away food to reheat in the pan during a busy week, while the pasta boils. It has only 5 ingredients and you can experiment with it. Put more carrots for a sweeter taste, try different tomato sauces, try ground beef, mix pork & beef or something rarer. It doesn't matter. Create your version. The secret lies in the time you let it simmer. It can be any time between 20 minutes and an infinite amount of hours. The longer, the better. We usually keep it simmering for at least 6 hours. Serve with pasta or zoodles (spiralized zucchini).

INGREDIENTS:

- Oil
- Onion
- Carrots
- Minced meat
- Tomato sauce

DIRECTIONS:

1. Chop the onion and carrots into fine pieces.
2. Heat the oil in a big pot, then add the chopped onion and the carrots.
3. When the onion is golden, add the minced meat and stir.
4. Stir and cook until the meat could be ready to eat, and that's when you cover the mixture with tomato sauce.
5. Cover with a lid and let it simmer as long as you wish. Every 3-4 hours you might want to add a bit of tomato sauce.
6. Serve warm or freeze for later use.

Make it extra: The Bolognese Sauce experience can be enhanced by adding herbs, different kinds of tomato sauces, or by adding some ingredients like bacon, sausage or mushrooms at the beginning. As is our mantra: experiment and be creative!

Paleo Zoodles with Tuna Sauce

Time: 10' prep + 10' cook (stirring) + 5' clean

This is an absolute favorite! Not sure how it was born, but it has been such a success that it's prepared in our kitchens almost every week. If you serve it without telling anyone this isn't real pasta, people will have a hard time believing you.

INGREDIENTS:

- Zucchini (2-3 per person depending on how big they are)
- Can of tuna, one per person. Better if tuna is in olive oil. (check for low-mercury tuna cans)
- Pesto Sauce (or basil + pine nuts + garlic and olive oil if you wish to make it yourself)
- Tomatoes, if you like them
- Olive oil

DIRECTIONS:

1. Spiralize zucchini (or cut into small/medium pieces).
2. Set the pot on the stove at medium to high heat.
3. When hot, add a drizzle of oil.
4. Add zucchini after 30 seconds.
5. While cooking, prepare the pesto on the side.
6. Remember to stir once in a while. If zucchini is burning, you'd want to lower the fire or add half a glass of water.
7. Add to your blender: garlic (as you like), 1 tablespoon oil, half a glass of water, basil, a handful of pine nuts, a pinch of salt.
8. When zucchini is soft, add fresh tomatoes (no need to cut).
9. Add tuna in cans after 30 seconds and mix.
10. Turn off the heat, add pesto sauce, and mix.
11. Serve. (Gentle reminder: rinse the bowl and the blender before eating. This saves you time for cleaning afterward.)

Make it extra: If you want it extra spicy, you can add fresh or dried chili peppers to the zucchini at the beginning.

The Student Pasta

Time: 1' prep + 15' cook + 3' clean

Italian students all over the world are cooking this pasta right now. It's a life-saver for those days where you forgot to go to the supermarket and the fridge lies literally empty. Worry not! You only need 3 main ingredients + pasta for this, and you most likely have them all in your kitchen already.

INGREDIENTS:

- Garlic
- Oil
- Chili peppers (fresh, dried, powder, whatever you can find!)
- Tomato sauce
- Salt & Pepper

DIRECTIONS:

1. Set a large pot of water to boil. Don't be shy, better a bigger pot than a small one. In the meantime, cut the chili peppers and garlic into small pieces.
2. When the water boils, season it with salt and cook the pasta.
3. Heat oil in a pan, add chili peppers and garlic, and cook until the garlic is golden. It only takes a couple of minutes, don't let it burn! Set aside.
4. When the pasta is ready (please read on the package the amount of time it takes to cook it and follow it!), drain, and add it to the pan.
5. Stir vigorously until the oil, garlic, and chili peppers are mixed well with all the ingredients.
6. Serve and sprinkle black pepper on top to give it some extra color and taste. Et voilà. No doubt the easiest pasta on the planet!

Make it extra: Parsley gives this pasta an even more colorful look, and tastes quite good, too! If you have it, add it together with the pasta at step 6.

Hot Tomato Sauce

Time: 2' prep + 15' cook + 3' clean

Better known as arrabbiata, hot tomato sauce is the adult version of the tomato sauce dish. The best part is that it's ready in less than 10 minutes! You can eat it with any pasta, but we often eat this with either zoodles (spiralized zucchini) or broccoli-based pasta.

INGREDIENTS:

- Pasta / zoodles
- Garlic
- Oil
- Chili peppers (fresh, dried, powder, whatever you can find!)
- Salt & Pepper
- Tomato sauce

DIRECTIONS:

1. Set a large pot of water to boil. Don't be shy, better a bigger pot than a small one.
2. In the meantime, cut the chili peppers and garlic into small pieces.
3. Heat the oil in a smaller pot, add chili peppers and garlic and cook until the garlic is golden. It only takes a couple of minutes, so don't let it burn!
4. Now add the tomato sauce and let it simmer for the remaining time until the pasta is cooked.
5. When the water boils, season it with salt, and cook the pasta (please read on the package the amount of time it takes to cook it and follow it!), drain.
6. Now pour the sauce over the pasta and stir until all the ingredients are mixed well.
7. Serve immediately with some parmesan on top if you have it.

Make it extra: You can turn this pasta into something completely different by adding bacon or olives, mushrooms, or your favorite vegetables. Be creative! If the chili peppers are too much for your liking, don't include them or simply reduce the amount.

Cheese Sauce with Black Pepper

Time: 2' prep + 15' cook + 2' clean

Not the healthiest of the recipes in this book, but a cheat meal is allowed once in a while right? Better known as cacio & pepe, this is the Italian version of Mac & Cheese and is hands down on another level. It also looks good and professional –so good you'll wonder how you didn't know about it before! You can eat it with any pasta, but we often eat ours with either zoodles (spiralized zucchini) or lentils-based pasta.

INGREDIENTS:

- Pasta / zoodles
- Black pepper
- Butter
- Salt
- Parmesan cheese
- Pecorino cheese

DIRECTIONS:

1. Set a large pot of water to boil. Don't be shy, better a bigger pot than a small one.
2. When the water boils, season it with salt, and cook the pasta in it.
3. In a pan, add the black pepper and toast for a few seconds. Add a knob of butter, cook until the butter melts, stir and set aside.
4. When the pasta is ready, drain but reserve a small quantity of hot water in a glass.
5. Add a little bit of the water to the butter-pepper mixture to create a richer sauce.
6. Add pasta and cover with cheese until it melts.
7. Serve immediately and garnish with extra parmesan and black pepper on top.

Make it extra: The secret of this pasta lies in its simplicity. For a little extra taste and work, try adding mushrooms in step 3 or tuna in step 6.

Prepare in a Minute, Check Back Later

The recipes in this section have four positive points in common:

1- You prepare them in less than 10 minutes.

2- You can eat several meals from it.

3- You can cook those recipes unattended, while you enjoy life.

4- They taste incredible! Turning you into a chef... with only a 10-minute effort!

We know, it sounds too good to be true, but there's only one way to find out: you gotta try them!

Pulled Pork

Time: 5' prepare + 5H cooking (unattended) + 5' clean

A couple of things: you need a dutch oven or a pot to roast the meat inside the oven for several hours. Also, you'll need some liquid to cook it in. The original recipe calls for beer, but we've successfully used apple cider or coke. Don't be afraid about the alcohol percentage or the sugar content, most of it will dissipate while roasting. The point is to flavor the meat. You could have pulled pork inside burritos, hamburgers, or as is, for a "naked" version as the main meat in the meal.

INGREDIENTS:

- Boneless pork shoulder (A lot! We use 1kg for 4 people.)
- Can of beer / coke / apple cider
- Salt & Pepper
- Oil
- Garlic
- Paprika and mustard powder (if you have it)
- Brown sugar (if you have it)

DIRECTIONS:

1. Preheat the oven at 250°F / 120°C.
2. In a bowl, mix a swirl of oil, crushed garlic, salt & pepper, and, if you have it, paprika and mustard powder and a bit of brown sugar and rub the mixture all over the pork.
3. Heat the dutch oven and sear the pork on all sides –only a few seconds per side: don't burn it!
4. Take the dutch oven off the stove. Now it's the time to add your preferred liquid all over and around the pork.
5. Cover with the lid and place the dutch oven inside the oven.
6. You can now leave it there for 4-6 hours, until it's so tender you can cut it with a fork, which is exactly what you're gonna do next.
7. Take the pork out, place it on a large plate, and shred it to pieces with two forks. You can add the excess liquid to keep the pork softer.
8. You can serve it right away or place it back in the dutch oven to keep warm until serving time.

Make it extra: To make it extra, you can add pretty much anything you like to the mixture before searing. Try, for instance, adding paprika powder, mustard powder, Sriracha sauce, Worcester sauce, Chipotle, brown sugar, Teriyaki, herbs... be creative!

Vegan Soup

Time: 15' prep + 3H cook (unattended) + 5' clean

In terms of time-saviour recipes, this is high on the list. We prepare this soup once every couple of weeks, freeze it in reusable boxes, and reheat whenever we're busy or don't have time to even cook for 20 minutes. In 5, it's ready. To prepare, it only takes chopping everything and adding them to boiling water. That's it. The ingredients are highly customizable and we vary them every time depending on what we need to get rid of or feel like eating. Like we say: be creative and experiment.

INGREDIENTS:

- Oil
- Zucchini
- Carrots
- Potatoes / Sweet potatoes
- Onion
- Broth dice
- Frozen Peas / Beans ...
- Salt

DIRECTIONS:

1. Set a lot of water to boil. We use the water boiler (twice).
2. Chop the vegetables quite coarsely. Keep only the onion on the side.
3. Heat oil in a large pot, add the onion.
4. When the onion is golden, add all the other vegetables, and stir for a few seconds.
5. Add to boiling water -enough to cover all the vegetables, and bring to a simmer.
6. Add the salt and vegetable broth dice, cover with a lid, bring to a simmer, then forget about it.
7. After about 3-4 hours, it's ready. You might want to add a bit of water if it evaporated too much.

Make it for the kids: Blend the vegetables once cooked, bring to a boil, add some pasta. The kids will love it... and it's healthy!

Low-Carb Chicken Pesto

Time: 5' prep + 20' cook (unattended) + 5' clean

This recipe is so easy your child can do it (ask them to help!). If you know what a caprese salad is, this is it, but on a chicken ...and in the oven. Ok, maybe it's not a caprese after all. But, the ingredients are quite similar. It's really easy to prepare, plus you can leave it in the oven to cook.

INGREDIENTS:

- Boneless chicken breasts
- Pesto
- Mozzarella
- Tomatoes
- Olive oil

DIRECTIONS:

1. Put the chicken pieces in a bowl.
2. Mix it with olive oil and salt & pepper.
3. Place the chicken on a baking sheet.
4. Cover the chicken with pesto.
5. Add slices of mozzarella to all chicken pieces.
6. Top them with slices of tomatoes.
7. Let it cook in the oven for 20 minutes at about 375°F / 180°C. This is a good time to clean the kitchen and set the table.
8. Turn off the oven, but keep the chicken inside for a couple more minutes.

Make it paleo and milk-free: Don't use mozzarella.

Greek Octopus

Time: 50' prep (not active) + 10' cook + 3' clean

Grilled octopus is one of the most famous dishes in Greek cuisine. Every respectable Greek restaurant has it on their menu. Today, it can also be on the menu of your home dinner. If you go directly to the grill, you end up with a chewy dish. The secret for a fantastic octopus is boiling it for 50 minutes before grilling. Aim at 3 tentacles per person.

INGREDIENTS:

- Octopus tentacles
- Oil
- Rosemary or parsley
- Garlic
- Salt & Pepper

DIRECTIONS:

1. Boil the octopus (set a 50-minute timer).
2. After boiling it, dry it.
3. Heat a dab of oil in a pan and sauté the octopus for 10 minutes.
4. Season it with rosemary, garlic, salt & pepper.
5. Cook or grill until the octopus is brown and tender.
6. Garnish with a slice of lemon if you have it.

Make it extra: We love it best when mixed in a fresh potato and tomato salad.

Chicken Broth

Time: 10' prep + 30' cook (unattended) + 3' clean

You can cook this one time and eat anytime throughout the week –as an appetizer or warming soup. It takes a couple of minutes to prepare, then just set the timer, and let it cook for a while.

INGREDIENTS:

- Chicken breasts
- Carrot
- Celery
- Onion
- Parsley if you have it
- Salt & Pepper

DIRECTIONS:

1. Coarsely cut the carrots, celery, and onion and put them in a large pot.
2. Add the chicken and cold water until it covers everything (and then some more, up until the rim of the pot is ok).
3. Bring to simmer and let it cook for 30' to a couple of hours.
4. Add salt & pepper to taste.
5. You can now preserve the broth in the fridge or freeze it and warm it up when needed.

Tip: The chicken and vegetables are great to eat too! Don't throw them away.

Latin American Ceviche

15' prep + 30' (marinate) + 5' clean

A classic dish from South America, ceviche is easy to prepare with no cooking involved. The fish marinates in lemon and is ready to eat without cooking. While it does take more than 30 mins, the actual time needed in preparing this is less than 15!

INGREDIENTS:

- Fish (Bass, Corvina, Tilapia, Snapper, Cod, Halibut)
- Red Onion
- Lime and Lemon
- Avocado
- Tomato

DIRECTIONS:

1. Squeeze in a bowl: 2 lemons and 1 lime per person.
2. Remove bones from the fish.
3. Cut the fish into very small cubes and put them in the lemon/lime juice. The smaller the pieces, the faster it will cook.
4. Cut the red onion into small pieces and add them. (For easier digestion, pre-immerse the onion in salt for 30 mins. Wash the salt away and add the onion back to the bowl.)
5. Let the fish cook in the lemon juice for 30-60 minutes.
6. While waiting, prepare a nice salad.
7. Cut avocados and tomatoes.
8. When the ceviche is ready, mix the salad with the fish.
9. (Add the onion if you put them in salt on step #4)

Tip: We highly recommend adding cilantro, especially if you don't have the gene that makes cilantro taste like soap.

Vegan Lentils and Spinach Soup

Time: 5' prep + 5' cook (active)
+ 20' (unattended) + 5' clean

Imagine: you come home from work in the evening, it's already dark outside. You're exhausted, even a little bit pissed at how late it is, and all you wish is for a shower and a creamy soup that'll wrap its flavors around you. Well, we can help with the soup part. While you take a shower it'll be ready!

INGREDIENTS:

- Coconut oil
- Coconut milk
- Red lentils (if you use dry lentils, you'll have to keep them in water either overnight or at least a couple of hours before starting)
- Fresh or frozen spinach
- Onion
- Salt & Pepper

DIRECTIONS:

1. Set a pan to medium heat and to it add a spoon of coconut oil.
2. Chop the onion into small pieces and add it to the pan.
3. Stir until the onion is golden.
4. Add the spinach and the lentils and stir until the lentils' liquid has evaporated (about 3-5 minutes).
5. Now you can cover everything with coconut milk, cover with a lid, bring to a simmer, and set a timer for about 20 minutes.
6. When the timer goes off, the soup is ready.
7. Season with salt and black pepper and serve.

Make it extra: We like to add ginger to the onion at the beginning to give it an extra rich flavor. To garnish, we add fresh cilantro, a couple of lime slices, and sometimes top it with basmati rice.

Enjoy the Snack

Okay, so getting in shape is the new "it". In the world of health and fitness, snacking in between meals has gained a bad rap. While we appreciate that it's not good for the health to keep reaching in the fridge (or food pantry) for frequent bites of food, this time we'd like to show you that snacks aren't absolutely a "no-no". Our recipes are great for kids, too. Really!

If you haven't tasted any of these amazing snack dishes, you're missing out on a healthy, yet mouthwatering, snacking experience. Give it a try!

Avocado Snack with Sea Salt

5' prep + (no cooking) + 2' clean

Our snack in the middle of a busy day.
To know if the avocado is just right, gently squeeze it with your hand. If it feels soft it's ready to eat. If hard, just leave it out on the kitchen counter for a day or two before it's ready.

INGREDIENTS:

- Avocado
- Oil
- Salt

DIRECTIONS:

1. Slice the avocado in half. Simply go around with your knife until you have cut the external part.
2. Remove the pit.
3. Once removed, each half gives you a nice space to sprinkle in all the ingredients.
4. Sprinkle the sea salt on top.
5. Add pepper or rosemary or any other spice (whatever you like).
6. Add oil and enjoy!

Make it smart: Buy plenty of avocados and keep some of them outside the fridge so they are slowly ripe.

Carrot Fries

Time: 5' prep + 40' cook (unattended) + 1' clean

Carrot fries are a healthy version of their potato counterparts. We use coconut oil, but if you don't wish to experiment with it, you can use olive oil. These are perfect snacks for parties (even kids love them), while watching TV, or just as a side dish.

INGREDIENTS:

- Carrots
- Salt & Pepper
- Coconut Oil

DIRECTIONS:

1. Preheat the oven at 400°F / 200°C.
2. Cut the carrots into wedge shapes.
3. Place on a baking sheet over an oven pan, coat with oil, salt & pepper.
4. Bake for 40 minutes or until slightly brown.

Make it extra: Add any herbs you like before baking.

Energy Bombs

Time: 8' prep + 0' cook + 2' clean

These energy bombs are a quick dessert that doesn't require any cooking. They are high on fat, making use of the goodness of coconut oil, so they're perfect for low-carb lovers out there.

INGREDIENTS:

- Walnuts
- Dates
- Coconut oil

DIRECTIONS:

1. Blend the walnuts. (Crash them if you don't have a blender.)
2. Add dates to the blender (same amount as walnuts).
3. Add a couple of spoons of coconut oil.
4. Blend all together.
5. Take them out of the blender and form them into little balls - the bombs.
6. Dip the bombs in your favorite garnish.
7. Freeze for 10 minutes.

Make it extra: Add vanilla, cocoa, coconut flakes, sesame seeds, pistachio, matcha, poppy seeds... experiment with the garnish!

Kale Chips

5' prep + 5' cook (oven) + 2' clean

If you think you don't like kale, you're going to change your mind after you try this one. When watching a movie on a Saturday night, this is the perfect snack. It's healthy – but go easy on the oil!

INGREDIENTS:

* Kale
* Oil
* Salt & Pepper

DIRECTIONS:

1. Turn on the oven at 375°F/180°C.
2. Clean the kale and remove its stems.
3. Keep the leaves as they are or gently make small pieces with your hands.
4. Set the leaves in a bowl and sprinkle with salt, pepper and oil. Mix.
5. Now, set the leaves on the baking sheet in the oven, making sure the leaves don't overlap. If you have more leaves than space, don't despair! Just make them in batches.
6. Bake for about 5 minutes and check. When you see the ends turning brown, that's your cue to take them out before they burn (and, oh boy, do they burn fast!).
7. Put them back in the same bowl and add any spice you might like.

Make it easy to clean: Dry the bowl with paper to absorb the oil and then wash it with soap.

Fried Pears

5' prep + 5' cook (active) + 2' clean

You're going to love this even if you don't like pears. We weren't big fans of pears until we tried this recipe. Pear, coconut oil and cinnamon, it's a weird combo, we agree. But we're here to promise you that the only risk here is that you'll get completely addicted to this snack.

INGREDIENTS:

- Pear
- Coconut oil
- Cinnamon

DIRECTIONS:

1. Slice the pear(s) into very thin slices. Aim for max length. Cut in half first, and then slice again.
2. Warm a pan on the stove and add at least a spoon of coconut oil. Spread it evenly and let it warm up for a few seconds.
3. Add the pear slices.
4. Fry them lightly for a few minutes.
5. Turn them every now and then, so they don't burn on one side.
6. When they get soft and slightly brown, remove from the pan.
7. Add cinnamon if you like it.

Make it extra: You can replace cinnamon with vanilla, or use both, or add anything else you like to the duo.

Smoother Than a Smoothie

Smoothies are the simplest of snacks as they require only three steps:
1- Chop
2- Blend
3- Drink

Though there are tens (or hundreds?) of different smoothies to choose from, these are the simplest and healthiest variations we drink and love —for their nutritional value. We usually keep a huge bag of frozen berries in the freezer to use with smoothies.

The secret to smoothies: add what you like and what you feel like adding. Try out different things to also change the smoothies' consistency. For example, you can try adding almond milk or orange juice if it's too thick. You can add chia seeds, cashew nuts, or almonds to make it thicker. Smoothies are yet another perfect expression of our kitchen principle: experiment and be creative!

Healthy Green Smoothie

Time: 5' prep + (no cooking) + 2' clean

Ah, the most hipster, instagrammable, healthy smoothie there is! Green smoothies are a great way to kickstart your day. This is also a perfect snack replacement for lunch or dinner.

INGREDIENTS:

- Almond milk / Greek Yoghurt
- Banana
- Ginger
- Apple
- Some frozen spinach and/or kale
- Lemon juice

DIRECTIONS:

1. Peel the bananas and put them into the blender.
2. Chop the apple and ginger coarsely, add to the blender.
3. Prepare and add the rest of the ingredients to the mixture and blend.

Make it extra: If you have it, add a tablespoon of chia seeds or crushed cashew as toppings.

Very Berry Smoothie

Time: 5' prep + (no cooking) + 2' clean

Both kids and adults love this wonderful violet smoothie: it's a real sweet treat! You can even freeze it and serve it as dessert.

INGREDIENTS:

- Blueberries, strawberries, any berries!
- Bananas
- Almond milk / Greek Yoghurt

DIRECTIONS:

1. Peel the bananas, put them into the blender.
2. Add everything else, too.
3. Blend.

Make it extra: Try adding mint leaves for a unique and special taste!

Sunshine Smoothie

Time: 5' prep + (no cooking) + 2' clean

Think hot Miami beaches. Golden sun up in the sky. You're thirsty. And, a little bit hungry. Hmmm...what's refreshing and tastes like summer?
A sunshine smoothie where the pineapple and orange juice will fill you with Vitamin C and happiness!

INGREDIENTS:

- Frozen pineapple chunks
- Bananas
- Orange juice
- Ice (if you have it!)

DIRECTIONS:

1. Peel the bananas, put them into the blender.
2. Squeeze the juice from the oranges and add it into the blender.
3. Add everything else, too.
4. Blend.

Make it extra: Add carrot juice if you can make one. Plus, ginger and lemon will add an extra unique taste to this smoothie, but it's not going to be that super easy anymore.

Morning Coffee Smoothie

Time: 5' prep + (no cooking) + 2' clean

Wait, what? Coffee smoothie? Is that a thing? It is now! We tend to prepare these on those hot summer mornings when we need to commute and want to enjoy something with a kick in it (coffee) but fresh (smoothie).

INGREDIENTS:

- Coffee
- Bananas
- Chia seeds
- Almond milk
- Ice

DIRECTIONS:

1. Peel the bananas and put them into the blender.
2. Add everything else, too.
3. Blend.

Make it extra: Try adding honey for extra sweetness, or some oat flakes for an extra creamy consistency.

Protein Smoothie

Time: 5' prep + (no cooking) + 2' clean

You want to get fit and hit those daily macros, but there are two problems: you want a sweet snack and the protein intake is too high. Solution: super simple protein shake. Will not lie, this is the most typical smoothie we have after working out in the afternoons.

INGREDIENTS:

- Blueberries, or strawberries, any berries!
- Protein powder
- Water

DIRECTIONS:

1. Put everything into the blender.
2. Blend.

Make it extra: Try adding a banana for extra magnesium. Your muscles will thank you for it the next day!

Masterclass: Risotto

Now that you have graduated from the easier recipes, it's time to get to the masterclass and try risotto.

The first time we tried a mushroom risotto, we couldn't finish the meal. Too much salt, too cooked, too everything. As any child wanting to go learn to ride a bike, we too tried and tried again, standing up every time we fell, and each time going a little bit further.

After many tries and many years, we now got the risotto recipes down.

So, buckle up, put your chef hat on, collect your ingredients, head to the kitchen, and get ready for a gastronomic experience that'll leave you wanting for more. Here we go!

Basic Risotto

Time: 5' prep + 25' cook (active) + 5' clean

Just think of the name 'risotto' and your mouth starts to water. You have a vision of an incredible dinner where your partner smiles at you with loving eyes. And all you did was a simple risotto. This basic risotto recipe is the starting point for many different variations.

INGREDIENTS:
- Oil & butter (if you have it)
- Onion & clove of garlic (if you have it)
- Risotto rice
- Vegetable broth
- Salt & Pepper
- Parmesan cheese (if you have it)
- Half a glass of white wine (if you have it)
- Parsley (if you have it)

DIRECTIONS:
1. Heat the broth, while in another pan heat a drizzle of oil and a knob of butter.
2. Cut the onion and the clove of garlic, then add them to the pan.
3. When the onion is golden (and the garlic hasn't burned), set a 2-minute timer, and add the rice. Stir continuously for these two minutes. Be careful they don't burn.
4. After 2 minutes, add white wine if you have it.
5. Add the broth. Cover the rice with it completely, stir, then cover with the lid.
6. Every few minutes, before the broth evaporates completely, add more broth, stir gently, and put the lid back on. You'll have to repeat this step until the risotto is ready. Taste it: it should be soft but not overcooked. Add salt & pepper to taste.
7. The risotto is ready in about 15 minutes (or whatever is written on the package!). When it's al dente, turn off the fire, add a knob of butter and parmesan cheese, stir, and let the pan sit with the lid on for another 3 minutes. If you want to show off to your friends, this last step is called mantecare: this is when you let the butter and parmesan sit to form an incredibly soft cream.
8. Garnish it with finely chopped parsley and serve warm.

Make it extra: If you're not a butter fan or you're out of parmesan, another way to make risotto creamy is to add a bit of fresh cheese instead.

Spinach Risotto

Time: 5' prep + 30' cook + 5' clean

This is one risotto that goes surprisingly well as a side dish or as a full meal. Also a favorite of the kids because "The green risotto is what Hulk eats to get stronger!" Yes, it was Popeye who ate spinach, but they're too young to know him and the result is the same!

INGREDIENTS:
- Oil & butter (if you have it)
- Onion & clove of garlic (if you have it)
- Spinach
- Risotto rice (about 200 g. for 2)
- Vegetable broth
- Salt & Pepper
- Parmesan cheese (if you have it)
- Half a glass of white wine (if you have it)

DIRECTIONS (You can recognize the 'Basic Risotto' directions.):
1. Heat the broth, while in another pan heat a drizzle of oil and a knob of butter.
2. Cut the onion and the clove of garlic, then add them to the pan.
3. When the onion is golden (and the garlic hasn't burned), add the spinach and stir.
4. When the spinach has cooked and doesn't have any extra water to them, set a 2-minute timer, and add the rice. Stir continuously for those two minutes. Be careful they don't burn.
5. After 2 minutes, add white wine if you have it.
6. Cover the rice with the broth completely, stir, then cover the pan with the lid.
7. Every few minutes, before the broth evaporates completely, add more broth, stir gently, and put the lid back on. You'll have to repeat this step until the risotto is ready. Taste it: it should be soft but not overcooked. Add salt & pepper to taste.
8. The risotto is ready in about 15 minutes (or whatever is written on the package!). When it's al dente, turn off the fire, add a knob of butter and parmesan cheese, stir, and let the pan sit with the lid on for another 3 minutes.

Make it extra: If you're not a butter fan or you're out of parmesan, another way to make risotto creamy is to add a bit of fresh cheese. You can also stir-fry chicken and add it at the end.

Risotto Milanese with Shrimps

Time: 5' prep + 25' cook (active) + 5' clean

This risotto's magic is in its cheerful, golden yellow color. That's where the saffron comes in. If you don't have any saffron, don't worry, it isn't a must! You can simply have a basic risotto recipe and add shrimps. Or, why not onion springs? Zucchini is a great addition to this dish, too. Experiment, try different ingredients, and make your version.

INGREDIENTS:
- Oil & butter (if you have it)
- Onion & clove of garlic (if you have it)
- Risotto rice (about 200 g. for 2)
- Vegetable broth
- Salt & Pepper
- Half a glass of white wine (if you have it)
- Shrimps
- Saffron

DIRECTIONS:
1. Heat the broth, while in another pan heat a drizzle of oil and a knob of butter.
2. Cut the onion and the clove of garlic, then add them to the pan.
3. When the onion is golden, set a 2-minute timer, and add the rice. Stir continuously for these two minutes. Be careful they don't burn.
4. After 2 minutes, add white wine if you have it.
5. Cover the rice with the broth, stir, then cover the pan with the lid.
6. Did you forget about the shrimps? We didn't! Heat a knob of butter or dab of oil in a frying pan and toss the shrimps in.
7. Now you will have to handle two pans at the same time, but luckily, the risotto basically cooks by itself. While you stir-fry the shrimps for a few minutes, check the risotto, too. Every few minutes, before the broth evaporates completely, add more broth, stir gently, and put the lid back on. You'll have to repeat this step until the rice is soft but not overcooked.
8. The shrimps cook in about 8 minutes. Add salt & pepper to taste, stir, and turn off the heat under the shrimps.
9. The risotto is ready in about 15 minutes (or whatever is written on the package!). When it's al dente, add the shrimps to the risotto, the saffron, a knob of butter, and stir until the yellow color is evenly distributed everywhere. Let the pan sit with the lid on for 3 minutes.
10. Garnish it with finely chopped parsley and serve warm.

Make it extra: Garnish it with arugula for the looks.

Creamy Risotto with Balsamico

Time: 5' prep + 25' cook (active) + 5' clean

This variation of the Basic Risotto is a star dish in many Italian restaurants. Its success lies in the swirl of different flavors that will explode in your mouth upon tasting. Be aware: when a saltier cheese mixes with sweet balsamic vinaigrette, your guests will ask for the recipe. This is the time for you to smile, wink, and keep your secret hidden.

INGREDIENTS:
- Oil & butter (if you have it)
- Onion & clove of garlic (if you have it)
- Risotto rice
- Vegetable broth
- Parmesan cheese
- Half a glass of white wine (if you have it)
- Black Pepper
- Balsamic vinaigrette

DIRECTIONS (You can recognize some of the 'Basic Risotto' directions.):
1. Heat the broth.
2. In a pan, heat a drizzle of oil and a knob of butter.
3. Cut the onion and the clove of garlic, then add them to the pan.
4. When the onion is golden (and the garlic hasn't burned), set a 2-minute timer, and add the rice. Stir continuously for those 2 minutes. Be careful they don't burn.
5. After 2 minutes, add white wine if you have it. The flavor-rich vapor will be marvelous!
6. Now it's time to add the broth. Cover the rice with it completely, stir, then cover the pan with the lid.
7. Every few minutes, before the broth evaporates completely, add more broth, stir gently, and put the lid back on. You'll have to repeat this step until the risotto is ready. Taste it: it should be soft but not overcooked.
8. The risotto is ready in about 15 minutes (or whatever is written on the package!). When it's al dente, turn off the fire, add a knob of butter and extra parmesan cheese, stir, and let the pan sit with the lid on for another 3 minutes. The butter and cheese will form an incredibly soft cream.
9. Upon serving, sprinkle black pepper and add extra parmesan on top, with a dash of balsamic vinaigrette.

Make it extra: Garnish it with a few half-sliced confit tomatoes to make it look even better!

Risotto ai Funghi Gourmet

Time: 10' to 3H prep + 30' cook (active) + 5' clean

The king of all risottos –and for a reason! It requires some extra love and care. You can use dried mushrooms or fresh ones. We usually mix dried porcini from Italy and whichever fresh mushroom we can find in the local store. If you use dried mushrooms, we suggest you start about 2 hours ahead to have the dish properly ready. Believe us, it's worth it!

INGREDIENTS:
- Oil & butter (if you have it)
- Onion & clove of garlic (if you have it)
- Risotto rice
- Vegetable broth
- Parmesan cheese
- Half a glass of white wine (if you have it)
- Dried or/and fresh mushrooms (Porcini if you can get them)
- Parsley

DIRECTIONS (If you won't use dried mushrooms, skip directions 1 & 2):
1. If you use dried mushrooms, you'll have to clean them first. Place the dried mushrooms in a bowl of lukewarm water for 30 minutes. Rinse the mushrooms, and repeat the process 3 times.
2. Cut the mushrooms into small pieces, set aside.
3. In a pan, heat a drizzle of oil and a knob of butter.
4. Cut the onion and the clove of garlic, then add them to the pan.
5. When the onion is golden (and the garlic hasn't burned), add the mushrooms and stir.
6. When the mushrooms are cooked for a few minutes (you could eat them by now), set a 2-minute timer, and add the rice. Stir continuously for those two minutes. Be careful they don't burn.
7. After 2 minutes, add white wine if you have it.
8. Cover the rice with the broth completely, stir, then cover the pan with the lid.
9. Every few minutes, before the broth evaporates completely, add more broth, stir gently, and put the lid back on. You'll have to repeat step 7 until the risotto is ready. Taste it: it should be soft but not overcooked.
10. The risotto is ready in about 15 minutes (or whatever is written on the package!). When it's al dente, turn off the fire, add finely-chopped parsley, a knob of butter and a lot of parmesan cheese, stir, and let the pan sit with the lid on for another 3 minutes. The butter and cheese will form an incredibly soft cream.

Risotto Pears & Walnuts

Time: 5' prep + 25' cook (active) + 5' clean

This fancy-looking risotto is one to surprise friends. It's a "basic risotto" plus two completely different, but complementary, ingredients.

INGREDIENTS:
- Oil & butter (if you have it)
- Onion & clove of garlic (if you have it)
- Risotto rice
- Vegetable broth
- Salt & Pepper
- Pears
- Walnuts
- Half a glass of white wine (if you have it)

DIRECTIONS (You can recognize some of the 'Basic Risotto' directions.):
1. Heat the broth and in a separate pan, heat a drizzle of oil and a knob of butter.
2. Cut the onion and the clove of garlic, then add them to the pan.
3. When the onion is golden (and the garlic hasn't burned), set a 2-minute timer, and add the rice. Stir continuously for those two minutes. Be careful else they burn.
4. After 2 minutes, add white wine if you have it.
5. Cover the rice with the broth completely, stir, then cover the pan with the lid.
6. Every few minutes, before the broth evaporates completely, add more broth, stir gently, and put the lid back on. You'll have to repeat this step until the risotto is ready. Taste it: it should be soft but not overcooked. Add salt & pepper to taste.
7. Now you have a few minutes to cut the pears into small pieces. Crush half of the walnuts also.
8. The risotto is ready in about 15 minutes (or whatever is written on the package!). When it's al dente, turn off the fire, add a knob of butter and the parmesan cheese, stir until the parmesan melts, then let the pan sit with the lid on for 1 minute.
9. Take the crushed walnuts and cut the pears, add them to the risotto, stir to mix the ingredients.
10. Garnish with a few full walnuts on top and, if you have it, a bit of grated lemon skin. Serve immediately.

Make it extra: If your diet allows it, a variation of this risotto includes gorgonzola cheese as well, in nice contrast with the sweetness of the pears.

89

Grazie and... BUON APPETITO!

Thank you for sharing your culinary journey with us. We hope the recipes in this book made you more passionate about cooking. They certainly help us every day in staying healthy with little time spent on cooking, while entertaining our families and friends.

As with everything in life, we're here for the journey, even if sometimes the end result is far from what's desired. Remember our little "rule"? **Experiment and be creative. Yup, you got it!**

While keeping in mind your specific nutritional need, freely add your style and your personality into the making of your dishes. Our recipes serve only as a general template. As for the ingredients and the cooking process itself, you have plenty of room to add, remove, decrease, replace, extend time, shorten the time, substitute, make mistakes, redo, etc.

Put on your cooking cap! Invite your partner and kids to add their flair in the making of a side dish, pasta, risotto, or smoothie... Turn your kitchen into a workshop of a memorable and exciting gastronomic masterpiece!

A Small Favour To Ask

We can't wait to hear from you.

- How did you like the book?
- Did we inspire you to cook?
- Do you have a recipe from this book you have already cooked twice?
- Which one was the most difficult?

We would really appreciate it if you could take a couple of minutes and leave a review on Amazon. You can also write to us with any feedback at **hello@youcanmake.it**.

If you cook any meal from this book, please tag us on Instagram **@foodforbusypeople.** Even if you make a mess and burn the entire thing, we would love to see it and hear from you!

Thank you once again.

Always Cook and Live with Love and Passion!

Ciao,
Claudio & Simone

About the authors

Simone Bocedi is born in Reggio Emilia, Italy, where he grew up on a steady diet of mountain bikes and football. He lived in different countries in Europe and finally settled in Finland, where he resides with his wife and two children. Very passionate about cooking, he's learned most of the tips you find in this book from his Mum –the most creative chef he's ever met. This book is a way for him to share some of his family's best-kept secrets with others.

Claudio Santori comes from a small Italian town called Serra San Quirico. Growing up in Italy, food has always been a very important part of his life, since Italians are already discussing dinner while eating lunch. He was vegetarian for 10 years, had a 5-year experience as a vegan, and since 2011 transitioned to a diet that's more Paleo/Low Carb/Keto. He wrote a book called "*Confessions of an ex Vegetarian*", narrating his journey from poor health to an outstanding physical state. Claudio is currently living in the United States with his wife –who makes the most amazing dishes and inspired a few included in this book.

Food for Lazy Busy People is the first book written together by Simone Bocedi and Claudio Santori.

The authors are also founders and owners of **You Can Make It** (www.youcanmake.it), a consulting company on personal development and business performance.

You can follow their personal growth stories on Medium (@youcanmakeit) or listen to their podcast, You Can Make It, available on podcast platforms worldwide.